Animal Fables and Other Tales Retold:
African Tales in the New World

Enid F.D'Oyley

Africa World Press, Inc.

P.O. Box 1892
Trenton, New Jersey 08607

First American Edition, Africa World Press, 1988

First published by Williams-Wallace Publishers, Canada, 1986

Africa World Press, Inc.
P.O. Box 1892
Trenton, N.J. 08607

ISBN: 0-86543-075-6
0-86543-076-4

Library of Congress Catalog Card No. 87-73226

PRINTED AND BOUND IN CANADA

ANANSI AND GOD

When the world was young, God who made everything lived in the sky, near to men, just above their heads. He told them that they could have whatever they wanted if they asked. And since God was so close, men became familiar with him, always demanding this or that, no matter how trivial. Women in need of an extra ingredient for their dinner would ask God, then tear off a piece of sky for their cooking pot. Children asked, then wiped their hands on the sky after they had eaten their meals.

At last God grew weary of their asking. He saw that he would be worn out with their demands. So he decided to separate himself from men, to remove his dwelling place, the sky, to a distance high above. And God, the Kindly One, the One on Whom Men Lean and Do Not Fall, took leave of men. Before he left, however, he told them to live in harmony with one another, to do no wrong. But if by chance they did wrong, he gave them a bird to sacrifice to him, in expiation for their wrongdoing. And to keep the link between heaven and earth, God commanded Anansi to spin a thread, exquisitely fine, that would reach up to the sky, his dwelling place. Then men would have a path to heaven should they seek it. God rewarded Anansi for his gift to men, and made him chief among men. After that God withdrew.

Now when Anansi was made chief among men, he became proud and presumptuous, and began to boast that he was more clever than God himself. "God could not even show men the way to heaven without my help," he vaunted.

God heard Anansi's foolish boast and was both angry and amused. He decided to put Anansi to the test. Summoning him into his presence, he told Anansi to bring him 'something' without telling him what the 'something', was. All day long, Anansi puzzled about the mysterious 'something', but at the end of the day he was no nearer knowing what God meant.

In the evening, God laughed until the tears ran down his cheeks, when Anansi, abashed, confessed that he could not do his bidding since he did not know what 'something' was.

"You boasted that you were more clever than God himself; prove it," God said, assuming once more a stern expression. Having spoken, he dismissed Anansi with a nod.

Thoughtfully, Anansi left sky for earth, to seek the 'something' God had commanded him to bring, knowing no more than when he had first been ushered into God's presence. Despair and humiliation began to creep upon him. Humbly he began to think that he was perhaps not so clever after all, when suddenly he had an idea. He called together all the birds in the land and borrowed from each a feather. With the feathers, he made a beautiful cloak of many colours which he draped over his body. Then he flew back to heaven where he perched in a tree near God's house.

In time, God came out of the house, and saw the brilliant bird of many colours perching in the tree. That was not his handiwork, he knew. Curious, he called together the council of gods to find out if they knew the name of the bird; if they were responsible for its being. None knew its name;

4

none knew whence it came. Then God sent the morning star to earth to seek its name. But no one knew it, not even the elephant who knew the names of all the creatures in the forest.

"Neither in heaven nor on earth is this bird's name known," the morning star reported when he had returned to heaven.

In the council of the gods, they pondered. Finally one of the gods suggested that they should ask Anansi. God, however, explained that he had sent Anansi on a mission, so he could not be consulted.

"What! Is this mission so important that he cannot be recalled?" they asked.

Then God told them how Anansi, becoming proud and presumptuous, had boasted that he was wiser than God himself, so he had set him the task of bringing him 'something'.

"Something!" exclaimed the gods, their eyebrows raised in surprise.

"Yes. Something." And, in a rash moment, God told them that the 'something' was the sun, moon, and darkness.

Anansi, in the tree, heard what God said. At once he flew from his perch, and when he was at a safe distance, he threw away his cloak of fine feathers. Then he set off to find the sun, moon, and darkness. But Anansi did not know where to find them, so he roamed aimlessly about, till realizing that he would never find them with his aimless wandering, he sought help. Now there was only one creature on earth that Anansi thought was perhaps wiser than he. That was the python.

Seven days and seven nights, Anansi journeyed to the farthest corner of the earth. There, apart from the dwelling place of men, he found the abode of the python.

"Tell me, Oh! Python," said Anansi, "where can I find the sun, moon, and darkness?"

The python with his thousand coils revolving round the earth, setting the sun, the moon, and the heavenly bodies in perpetual motion, looked with wise eyes at Anansi.

"You know not what you ask," said the python, trying to dissuade him. But Anansi held firm. He wanted the sun, moon, and darkness to take to God and nothing could keep him from his purpose.

Gravely the python looked at Anansi; gravely he shook his head. "The sun and moon, Lisa and Mawu, are heavenly twins, brother and sister, born of God himself," he said gently. "They cannot be touched by man."

Anansi, on hearing this, was more determined than ever. If he should take the heavenly twins to God, then it would prove beyond a doubt that he was the cleverest being alive. So he repeated his wish.

5

The python saw that Anansi would not be dissuaded, and giving him a bag, he told him to travel eastward to the place where the sun dwelt. "Await the moment when he first steps out of his house, a faint blush. Lift your hands on high in adulation, stretch out the bag and so you will gather him in. But mark well; should you miss that moment, he becomes too fierce and strong to be contained within a bag and he will be gone forever.

"From there go westward where Mawu the moon dwells remote, high above the highest mountain. Hold aloft the bag as if in ritual offering, and when first she appears seize her. Choose well the moment for she is shy and elusive." So spoke the python to Anansi.

The python paused. "Tell me where darkness is to be found," prompted Anansi as the python remained silent.

"The bat holds the answer to that, yet he knows not," replied the python, shaking his head. "God has entrusted him with the basket containing darkness to take to the moon. Get it from him, if you can." On saying that he closed his eyes and went to sleep.

Swiftly Anansi set out to find the sun. Earnestly he did as the python bade him, and when the sun emerged, fresh from his bed, Anansi succeeded in luring him into his bag. From there, he travelled westward to the dwelling place of the moon. The way was long and rough, uphill all the way. As he stumbled along with his bag, puffing at every breath, he spied the bat a short way ahead of him, weighted down with a basket on his back. Anansi, glad to have company, hastened to overtake him. Then he slackened his pace when he saw that the bat was taking the basket from his back to put under a tree. Afterwards he flew away. Thankfully, Anansi snatched up the basket, stuffed it in his bag without so much as a 'by your leave', and hurried on his way, leaving the bat to chase about in every direction seeking the basket.

Anansi found the moon, caught her, then returned to heaven, jubilant.

"You have been a long time," God said to him, "Have you brought the 'something'?"

"Yes," said Anansi, taking the basket out of his bag. God recognized the basket containing darkness, and as Anansi was giving it to him, it fell and flew open. And darkness escaped and descended upon men on earth so that they could not see. Yet it was not God's wish that darkness should escape, and rove uncontrolled. So when Anansi drew the moon from his bag, God gave her pre-eminence over darkness. Then men on earth could see in a twilight haze. Finally when Anansi took out the sun, he was so splendid, so brilliant that he completely overshadowed his sister, the moon. And some men on earth saw his splendour and became blinded by it. But some had their eyes shut and did not see, so they came to no harm.

Then God decided to establish forever the domain of the heavenly pair. He set the moon, holding darkness in her hands, to rule the night with her cool and gentle light, and the sun, brilliant and strong, to rule the day. The moon he endowed with the wisdom of age, but to the sun he gave the vigour and fierceness of youth. As for Anansi, God was so pleased with the way in which he had performed his task that, forgetting his anger, he made him the cleverest of men, warning him however to cease his boasting and end his arrogance.

Anansi promised. But he did not always remember his promise, and whenever he became too presumptuous, he was punished.

HOW THE LEOPARD GOT ITS SPOT

In the beginning when the world was very young, the Leopard and Fire were friends. Fire was, at that time still a newcomer to earth. For after the Creator, maker of all things had divided the universe among his children, there arose a dispute between Earth and Sky about who was greater. Earth, being the elder, claimed pre-eminence by virtue of seniority. Said he to Sky:

"You are a callow youth, loud and brash — a veritable braggart. And you compensate for your lack of years, by swaggering about as if you own the universe."

"And you," bellowed Sky, "are such a mealy-mouthed nincompoop, that no one pays the least attention to you. Why, when I speak everyone takes notice." And to illustrate his point, he let his thunder roll, so that the very foundations of the universe were shaken, and he let his lightning flash blinding tongues of fire.

Earth, startled jumped out of his seat like a jack-in-the-box, and covering his ear, he ran off to cower in a corner.

Sky, satisfied that he had intimidated Earth enough, laughed a great laugh that echoed through the vaults of the universe. He was such a loud fellow that he could never do anything without creating a din.

Earth, there and then decided that in order to avoid further quarrels, he would gather up his inheritance and go below. Like a dutiful child, however, he discussed his plan with the Creator.

"An excellent idea," the Creator agreed. Naturally he was disturbed by the constant bickering of Earth and Sky. "You shall be like the two halves of a calabash," the Creator said. "Sky will remain above, and, yes, you may go below. Now mind you! No fighting!"

At those words, Earth hastily stuffed all his inheritance in a great sack and went below.

"What has that to do with "How the Leopard got its Spot," you ask. That's the story, isn't it?"

Well, for a time after Earth went below, everything was peaceful and calm. Everyone was happy and friendly. But that happy state did not last. Soon the birds, the insects, the animals and all living creatures began to grumble. They could not keep warm no matter how hard they tried, they said to Earth, their king. And to make matters worse, they were dying from thirst, since no rain had fallen for three whole years, they complained.

Earth, concerned at their unhappiness, went to consult the Oracle.

"Sky is angry, very angry, and has withheld rain, because you took all the inheritance," said the Oracle.

Then Earth remembered. He had taken everything except Fire and Water, because there was no place for them in the sack he had taken below. How short-sighted he had been to have left them! he berated himself. Now Sky had them. How could he get them for his people?

He scratched his head in thought. Perhaps he had been a bit greedy to have taken all the inheritance. Stupid too, not to have realized how important Fire and Water were! But they seemed so insignificant.

"What shall I do?" he asked the Oracle.

"Make a sacrifice of your possessions. Give up some of the inheritance, then send a bird to Sky to tell him. And so he will be appeased."

Earth did as he was told. Sky accepted his overtures of friendship.

"Tell Earth," he said to the bird, "that I hold no grudge against him, for even though he took all the inheritance, I was able to get them back by simply controlling Fire and Water." And as a sign of reconciliation, he gave a clap of thunder and sheets of rain began to fall.

You may be sure that Earth no longer thought Sky boisterous and boastful.

But Sky did not send Fire. Knowing its power, he was zealously guarding it for himself alone. Earth spent many days and nights thinking how he could get Sky to share Fire with him. Then one day when he had almost given up hope of ever finding an answer, the Mason-Wasp came to see him.

"The birds, insects, animals and all living creatures are tired of being cold. We need Fire," said the Mason-Wasp.

"Sky is guarding it for himself, alone," said Earth. "Nothing that I do, not my sacrifices, nor my pleadings, will make him share it with us."

"Then we should implore the Creator of all things, the Giver of all Gifts, to intervene on our behalf," said the Mason-Wasp. "I, myself, will go to him to ask for Fire, if someone will go with me."

Earth looked at the Mason-Wasp, with its delicate blue wings, its yellow middle and its striped legs. Delicate and beautiful; but strong? He wondered.

Nevertheless, he was desperate enough to be willing to try anything. So he gave his blessing to the Mason-Wasp, the eagle, the vulture, and the crow, who had volunteered to accompany him.

"Farewell," they called, as they flew skyward.

"Ten days later, some bones fell to the earth; they were the bones of the vulture. Ten more days went by, and the bones which fell were those of the eagle. Finally the small bones of the crow whitened the earth. The Mason-Wasp was now alone.

Alone, he flew for thirty days, resting on the edge of the clouds, but never managing to reach the top of the Sky where the Creator lived.

The Creator heard the Mason-Wasp and came down from his dwelling place to ask him where he was going.

"I am seeking the Creator, Giver of all Gifts, to ask for Fire, but I cannot find him. My friends have all fallen by the way, and I am left alone," the Mason-Wasp said.

The Creator took pity on him, so delicate, so small yet so courageous. He knew that Sky was selfish to keep Fire for himself, alone.

"Return to Earth," he said, "and build there a house with a fireplace. Build it well with sticks and stones. Near the fireplace build your nest."

The Mason-Wasp returned to Earth and did as the Creator commanded. In the morning when he awoke, he found Fire sitting in the fireplace. And the Mason-Wasp was warm, as he had never been before. Jubilant, he proclaimed to all:

"Fire is come to Earth!"

Then the birds, the insects and all living creatures, curious, came to see Fire and to welcome him. Warm they left; warm as they had never been before. Then all the living creatures rewarded the Mason-Wasp for bringing Fire to earth, by making him its guardian. And ever after he built his nest near to the fireplace, because the Creator had told him to do so.

Soon the House of Fire became the most popular spot on earth, and Fire, the most popular of people. None came more frequently to the House of Fire than the Leopard. Everyday he went to see Fire, and in time a fast friendship developed between the two. But Fire never returned the visit; he never went to the Leopard's house.

"What sort of a friend is that, who never returns a visit," the Leopard's wife mocked him. "That's a one-sided friendship, I'd say."

The Leopard paid no attention to her words; he continued to visit Fire day after day. And when he returned from his daily visit, his wife would taunt him. "I'll tell you why Fire does not visit our house; he thinks it too poor and unworthy."

The Leopard listened in silence until one day he felt that he had had enough. To prevent his wife from goading him to death, he invited Fire to visit his house.

Fire thanked him for his invitation, but regretted that he could not accept it, since he never visited.

"If even for a few seconds, please," the Leopard pressed him.

"Thank you very much, but I never walk," Fire said, "so I cannot come to your house."

"You are full of excuses, my friend," said the Leopard, who was beginning to feel that his wife was perhaps right.

Fire looked at him sadly and sighed. "As you wish it, so it will be. I will come to your house; but first I need a road of dry leaves from my house to yours."

The Leopard went home and told his wife what Fire had said. Gladly, she gathered dry leaves and laid them in a straight line from her house to the house of Fire. Then she went indoors, and singing under her breath as she worked, she and her husband prepared their home to receive their guest.

As they were putting the finishing touches to their preparations, they heard the sound of a mighty rushing wind, and a crackling sound at their door. The Leopard hastily went to the door to see what was the matter.

Fire he saw at the door, forcing his way in; and his fingers of flame touched the Leopard. Frightened, he leapt backwards; his wife did likewise. And as Fire entered the house, consuming everything in his path, the Leopard and his wife jumped through the window and were saved.

His wife now truly wise said, "It is the nature of Fire to burn, no matter what," as she sadly surveyed the marks all over their bodies — black spots where the fingers of Fire had touched them.

THE TORTOISE AND THE FRUIT

Long ago, and long ago, there was a great famine in the land. No rain fell from the heavens; the water holes and the rivers dried up; the grass withered on the parched and cracked ground, and the animals wasted away from lack of food.

In despair, they looked at all the trees in the woods in search of food; but none yielded fruits. All were withered and bare. All except one. One which grew deep in the heart of the woods. Tall and straight it was, full of juicy ripe fruits, dark purple, tempting. Day after day, they looked with longing eyes at the tree laden with fruits.

"What is it? What is its name?" they asked one another, and would not eat of the fruit, for they did not know its name.

And every day they became thinner and thinner as they panted for water and hungered for food.

They cried to Shango for help; Shango, God of Thunder and Lightning, Shango, God of the Great Rivers, Mediator in the Council of Gods. For with lightning and thunder would come the rains, and with the rains, the grass would grow again, the earth come to life, the rivers and water holes become swollen with water, and then they would have enough to eat.

But Shango did not answer their cries. The drought continued and the animals became weaker and weaker, almost too weak to offer their daily prayer.

"He does not answer our prayers. He is deaf to our pleas," they said in disappointment. "Perhaps our cries do not reach heaven. Let us make sacrifice to Great God," they said. "We may have done some wrong."

They made a ritual offering of the hen and the pigeon; they being the first creatures taken by Great God to earth when it was only a marshy and watery waste. But Great God paid no heed, and the famine continued.

Then the monkey, thin and wasted as his companions, resolved to go to heaven to ask the name of the fruit that grew on the tree, deep in the heart of the woods. He would ask it of the great Shango himself, God of Thunder and Lightning, God of the Great Rivers, Mediator in the Council of Gods.

Full of hope, he set out on his journey. How he reached heaven, it is not told. What he said to Shango is not known. But joyfully, he started on the return journey to earth knowing the name of the fruit, and repeating it to himself along the way:

> Mussa, mussa, mussa,
> mussangabira, mussa.

He had not gone far before he met a witch. In order to confuse him, she began to sing:

> Munga, Selenga, ingabela,
> Vina, quivina, vinam.

The monkey kept repeating to himself:

> Mussa, mussa, mussa,
> mussangabira, mussa.

And the old witch kept on chanting at the top of her voice:

> Munga, selenga, ingabela,
> Vina, quivina, vinam.

At last the poor monkey became confused: "Mu ... mu ...," he repeated, struggling to remember the name of the fruit. And although he called on the help of the powerful Shango, he ended up forgetting it. Sadly, he returned to the village, his mission a failure. Sadly his companions welcomed him home, their hopes dashed.

The animals were, however, convinced that only by learning the name of of the fruit could they be saved. They gathered together in a circle around the tree laden with fruits.

"Who will go to the great Shango, God of Thunder and Lightning, God of the Great Rivers, Mediator in the Council of Gods, to ask the name of the fruit?" they asked. Like an echo, the question went round the circle, "Who will go to the great Shango ...?"

They looked weakly at one another, faint from hunger. Which of them had the strength and courage to undertake such a long and arduous journey? They looked at one another. Thinking ... waiting.

At last the hare volunteered. Cheered by the good wishes of his companions, he sped on his way. Time went by, and the animals waited and hoped. But the hare returned, equally defeated. The wicked witch had succeeded in confusing him, as she had confused the monkey. After that, each animal that went met the same adventure and suffered the same fate. There was no escaping the wicked witch.

Then the tortoise offered himself. Slow at the best of times, he had become even slower from starvation. His fellow creatures wondered if indeed he would be able to make that journey to heaven. But in their great need they clung to every hope, however small. The tortoise, not at all daunted, courageously set out to find the great Shango. How many false turns he took! How many times, overcome with weariness, almost fainting from hunger, he felt like turning back!

But a voice urged him on: "Only by learning the name of the fruit will you and your companions be saved." So the tortoise dragged one weary foot after another, slowly and surely, till at last, faint and travel-worn, he reached heaven. The great Shango, sitting on his throne, breathing fire when he spoke, asked:

"From whence do you come, O little one?"

"From the land of famine, from a land parched with drought, where animals with tongues lolling to catch a drop of rain that will not fall, despairingly lie down to die." So spoke the tortoise in a brave voice.

Shango marvelled at the courage of the little tortoise, braving his fiery breath, the breath with which he could slay thousands. He took pity on the weakened condition of his creatures.

13

"What would you have, my little one?" he breathed.

"Tell me, O mighty Shango, all-powerful one. Tell me the name of the fruit which flourishes, even in the height of the longest drought. Tell me its name that we may eat and not die."

"It is not my wish that you should die," said Shango, breathing the name of the fruit, through fire, as he had done so many times before.

Satisfied, the tortoise joyfully set out on the return journey, repeating the name:

Mussa, mussa, mussa,
mussangabira, mussa.

The wicked witch was lying in wait for the tortoise. She jumped out into the middle of the road and began to sing her old song, in order to confuse him, just as she had done with all the other creatures before him. But the tortoise was not disturbed, he just kept on saying the name to himself.

The old witch was furious. She angrily grasped him with clawlike hands and threw him to the ground. Quickly, the tortoise got up and, moving about, he shouted:

Arre, salta, Cerce, bize!

or in plain language, "Get along, you wicked witch!" This he said and repeated the name of the appetizing fruit. So he continued, scaring off the wicked witch and repeating the name, until he triumphantly arrived home.

And so it was, from that time on, the animals could eat the fruit of the tree which up to then had been nameless, thanks to the tortoise. But in the struggle with the witch, the tortoise broke his beautiful shell when he fell, and since then, the tortoise wanders throughout the world with cracks in his shell.

THE KEBUNGO, THE DOG, AND THE HARE

Once upon a time, when animals roved the world in perfect freedom, there lived a strange creature called the Kebungo. Part animal, part man, he had an enormous head, and a hole in his back, just like a pocket. Every year at a certain time, he used to make his rounds of houses to snatch unwary children. These he would store in his pocket to gobble up afterwards.

Now the dog had many children who were always being eaten by the ferocious Kebungo. So that when the time was drawing near for the Kebungo's visit, she thought of a way to try to save those that remained. She decided to dig a hole in the ground, and after putting her children in it, she would sit on it. The time came. She did as she had planned, but not before she had dressed herself very coquettishly in a skirt of many colours, and adorned herself with rows and rows of necklaces.

When the Kebungo saw the dog dressed in this fashion, he did not recognize her, and he was afraid to get close to her.

At that moment, a rabbit happened to pass by. The Kebungo seized the opportunity to ask: "Friend, do you know who that stranger is?"

"I do not know, friend," replied the rabbit, hopping by.

The Kebungo asked the same question of a fox when she went by, and also of many other creatures without anyone knowing the answer. Finally, the monkey, laughing, said to him: "But, friend, is it possible that you do not know the dog disguised in skirt and necklace?"

Enraged at being duped, the Kebungo began to chase the dog and her children. But the dog began to pursue a hare that was passing by at that moment. And so at full speed, they entered the city, the Kebungo chasing the dog, and the dog the hare. There, Man put an end to the dispute. He captured them all, and put them to work. But from that day on, dogs chase hares wherever they are found. And as for the Kebungo, Man worked him so hard that as soon as he could he escaped and was never heard of again.

THE KEBUNGO AND THE BOY WITH
THE BAG OF FEATHERS

There was once a little boy whose favourite game was gathering feathers. He spent his days collecting feathers of all the birds he could find, large and small, and storing them in a bag. One day he went for a walk with his family, his father, mother, brother and sister, to an isolated place near a large dark forest. In that desolate place, the villagers said, the Kebungos were accustomed to meet. The boy, not really wanting to go for the walk, carried his bag with him, because he planned to collect more feathers on the way.

Shortly after they reached the place, they heard a blood-curdling sound which seemed to be coming from the depths of the earth. "It is the Kebungo! It is the Kebungo!" they cried, trembling in terror.

Before they had time to think, the little company scattered and ran like feathers caught in the wind, all save the boy who stood firm. Bravely, he urged them to stop running and to form a line. Encouraged by his calm manner, the father, the mother, the brother, and the sister, stopped their aimless running and formed a line, holding hands.

16

To each of them, the boy gave a fan made with the feathers from the wings of large birds, and another with those from the tails of small birds. He himself had shaped the fans with the feathers collected the previous day. By the time he had arranged everything to his satisfaction, the Kebungo was well upon them.

The Kebungo was a fearful creature to behold, with his enormous, human-looking head, the pouch on his back and his cloven hooves. Fearfully, they wondered if they had been wise in remaining. Fearfully, they wondered if the boy's plan could save them.

As the Kebungo approached them, breathing terror, cloven hooves raised to trample them, the first person in the line began to sing the song which the boy had taught him:

> That is my father, ay!
> Ganzaru, you fall, or you don't fall.

The song had scarcely ended before the fans he had in his hands opened and carried him flying to lodge in a nearby tree. With an angry roar, the Kebungo retreated, amazed.

When his fear had passed, he again approached with raised hooves to trample the second person in the line. At once, she began to sing the song the boy had taught her:

> That is my mother, ay!
> Ganzaru, you fall, or you don't fall.

Before the song had well ended, her fans also opened and carried her flying into the nearby tree.

And so it happened with the others in the line. Their fans also opened and carried them flying into the tree.

Next, the Kebungo reached the boy, and attempted to snatch him. But the boy had made wings for himself with his feathers. Secretly, too, he had joined together his relatives' fans to his wings. He gave a gentle tug, and lifted himself off the ground, in full flight towards his house, with his family in tow, supported by their fans.

So happy were they at having saved themselves from the ferocious Kebungo, that when they had arrived safely in the village, they dug a large hole at the entrance to it, which they covered with leaves. Hiding themselves in their house, they awaited the monster who came running in pursuit of them. He came so hurriedly, that he did not see the concealed hole and he fell in.

The other Kebungos learned from that lesson and took fear ... so much so, that they were never seen again.

THE TORTOISE AND THE ELEPHANT

In the quiet of an afternoon, when the tortoise and the rhinoceros, the hippopotamus, the crocodile and all the other animals were taking their rest by the water hole, the tortoise, or 'bald-headed witch' as everyone called her, suddenly pushed her head outside her shell and said: "Guess what! I can make the elephant act like a horse."

They all began to laugh and to make fun of the tortoise. Noisily they shouted: "Come on, now ... You can't make an elephant your horse. Not on your life ... Not at all!"

"Of course, I can," she replied confidently. "And I will make you a bet. I will enter the city riding on an elephant."

18

The rhinoceros, the hippopotamus, the crocodile and all the other animals accepted the bet. They were so sure it could never happen.

The tortoise left for the woods to seek the elephant.

"Dear friend," she said, when she had found him, "all the animals go about saying that you do not go to the city because you are very ugly and ungainly."

"They are some fools. If I do not go, it is because I prefer to remain here where it is quiet," said the elephant, clearly annoyed. "Besides," he added as an afterthought, "I do not know the road to the city."

"Oh, if it is only for that," replied the tortoise, 'bald-headed witch', "come with me. I will show you the way, and then you will see how all the animals will be sorry for being so unkind."

The elephant agreed. The two set out on the journey to the city. For every step the elephant took with his lumbering walk, the tortoise had to take seven; her legs were so short. When they were near the city, the tortoise said in a weary voice: "Dear friend, you do walk very fast, and I am so tired from trying to keep up with you. Won't you let me climb on your back?"

"Of course. Why not?" said the elephant and at once he kneeled so that his friend could climb on his back.

After they had travelled like that for a while, the tortoise said: "Look, friend, when I tickle your back you must run ... and when I strike you on the head you must run even faster ... so that you can make a triumphant entry into the city."

"Agreed," said the elephant who was thinking only of getting to the city as fast as possible.

On arriving near the city where the animals were, the tortoise, 'bald-headed witch', tickled the elephant, and he began to run. Then soon afterwards she struck him lightly on the head. The elephant began to run even faster as had been agreed. When the rhinoceros, the hippopotamus, the crocodile, and all the other animals saw that, they could not believe their eyes. At the same time the tortoise shouted to them: "Didn't I tell you that I would enter the city riding on the elephant as if it were a horse?"

"Wait a minute! What's that? What do you mean by that ... as if I were a horse?" the elephant exclaimed furiously.

"Nothing, dear friend, it was only a joke!" replied the tortoise meekly.

But the elephant was no fool. He saw that all the animals were peeping through the doors and windows of their houses, looking at him and laughing. At that he became even more furious.

"I am going to throw you against the stones and break you into a thousand pieces, traitor!" the elephant fumed.

"Good! That's not such a bad idea after all ... throw me there if you must. In fact, that is what I wish. And don't pity me either, for I surely will not die. Because in order to kill me, you will have to take me where there is a lot of mud ... to drown me."

The elephant believed her, and began to run towards a swampy spot, where he shook her off his back. He raised his legs to crush her into a thousand pieces, but the clever tortoise submerged herself in the mud on one side and came out on the other.

As she came out on the other side, she shouted so that the rest of the animals could hear her: "Didn't I tell you that I was going to enter the city riding on my good old friend?"

The elephant, on seeing that he could not silence the tortoise, 'bald-headed witch', returned to his country, the woods. There he joined the other elephants and told them what had happened to him.

"It is your fault," they replied. "You were crazy even to want to enter the city, and crazier still to bear the tortoise on your back."

A little sadder and wiser from his experience, the elephant agreed. And this is why, from that time on, elephants never go near cities.

THE MONKEY AND HIS TAIL

A monkey sat disconsolate by the side of a deserted highway, thinking. Bored with playing his usual tricks, he tried to find new ways to amuse himself. He thought of one trick after another, but none succeeded in lifting the gloom from his face. He stretched and yawned, and began playing with his tail from sheer boredom, when suddenly he spied a man driving a cart loaded with razors.

At once, a mischievous light came into his eyes as he rapidly thought of a plan. Swiftly, he placed himself in the middle of the road, and stretched out his tail exactly at the point where the man would pass with his cart. As the man drew nearer and nearer, the monkey asked him to take another path.

"Take your tail out of the way," said the man, driving his cart straight along the road, without swerving to the right or to the left.

"I won't," replied the monkey, blinking.

"Come on, get out of my way so that I can pass," the man said in an annoyed voice.

"I was here first," smugly asserted the monkey.

They argued back and forth for some time, and when the man saw that he was getting nowhere with the monkey who was looking slyly at him from under hooded eyes, he angrily drove his cart over the tail. In so doing, he cut it off with the wheels.

Immediately, the monkey began to howl. "I want my tail! I want my tail!" he shrieked. "Give me back my tail, or give me a razor!" He carried on at such length that, in order to get him to shut up, the man agreed to give him a razor.

Contented, the monkey went singing on his way

I lost my tail, I gained a razor;
Tinglin, tinglin, to Angola I'm going!

Further along the road, he met an old man making baskets. He was cutting reeds for the baskets with his teeth. The mischievous monkey stopped and said in a sympathetic voice: "Poor old man ... cutting reeds with your teeth ... Here! Take my razor."

Gratefully, the old man accepted; but as he was cutting a reed, the razor broke.

At once, the monkey began to cry: "I want my razor! I want my razor! Give me back my razor or give me a basket!"

Despairing that the monkey would ever shut up, the old man handed him a basket. Happily, the monkey went away, singing to the four winds:

I lost my tail, I gained a razor;
I lost my razor, I gained a basket;
Tinglin, tinglin, to Angola I'm going!

Shortly afterwards, he came across an old woman who was making bread and storing the loaves in her lap. On seeing her, he ran up to her. Gently, he said: "Oh, my lady, making loaves without having any place to store them. Here! Have my basket!"

She thanked him for his kindness and began to gather up the loaves in the basket. But she put so many in, that the basket burst.

Tearing his hair in mock rage, the monkey cried: "I want my basket! I want my basket! Give me back my basket or give me a loaf!"

The old woman was so frightened at his tantrum, that she gave him a nice hot loaf.

The fun-loving monkey, using the loaf as a flute, went away dancing as he sang:

> *I lost my tail, I gained a razor;*
> *I lost my razor, I gained a basket;*
> *I lost my basket and gained a loaf.*
> *And this loaf I am going to eat up;*
> *Tinglin, tinglin, to Angola I'm going!*

THE MONKEY BUYS CORN

Once upon a time the monkey wanted to buy corn for his dinner. But he had no money. Not any. So he went to his friend, the cock.

"Friend cock," he said, "will you sell me a handful of corn now, and let me pay for it tomorrow?"

"With pleasure," said the cock. He gave the handful of corn to the monkey who then took leave of him and went to the house of his friend, the fox.

"Friend fox," he said, "would you mind selling me a handful of corn now and waiting until tomorrow for the payment?" The monkey named the same day on which he had agreed to pay the cock, but half an hour later.

"Gladly," said the fox, giving him a handful of corn. The monkey thanked him and from there he went to the house of his friend, the dog, whom he asked for the same amount of corn that he had bought from the cock and the fox. He promised to pay his debt on the same day on which he had agreed to pay the other two, but allowed half an hour after the time for the fox.

As the monkey was still not satisfied, because he had not got all the corn that he needed for his dinner, he went to see the tiger, who also gave him a handful of corn, on credit. They arranged that the tiger would collect payment on the same day as the cock, the fox and the dog, but half an hour after the latter. The tiger also agreed, as the others had before him, to go to the monkey's house to collect the debt.

Fully satisfied, the monkey went back to his house, where he prepared a great feast for himself. He ate so much that he became quite ill, or so he pretended to be.

The next day came; the day when he had promised to pay for the corn. First came the cock, knocking at his door.

"Come in," said a feeble voice. The cock entered. He found the monkey sitting up in bed, groaning pitifully, saying he was in terrible pain.

Nevertheless he was very courteous. He invited the cock to rest for some minutes. Then he invited him to partake of the meal he had prepared with the corn he had bought. The cock ate.

"What a delicious meal!" he exclaimed in delight, after he had eaten.

Just then, the fox knocked at the door. The cock, on spying the long nose of the fox, became very frightened. But the monkey calmed him. "You may hide under my bed," he said. Quickly, the cock hid, and none too soon, as the fox pushed his way into the room. He, too, was invited to eat some of the dinner the monkey had prepared.

"How tasty!" he said, licking his lips.

"Our friend, the cock, also found it tasty," said the monkey.

"What! Did that fellow go by here?" asked the fox.

"Yes, but he left a long time ago," replied the trickster of a monkey, pointing under the bed as he spoke.

Without waiting to hear any more, the fox hurled himself under the bed. A bloody battle took place between the cock and the fox, in which the fox came out victorious. He ended it by gobbling up the cock.

Right at that moment, the dog knocked at the door. The same scene was repeated. But this time the dog was the one who won; and he ate up the fox.

Afterwards the tiger came to the door. He was invited in; he enjoyed the monkey's dinner; he fought with the dog and was the victor. When he had finished eating up the dog, he asked the monkey to settle his account.

The foolish monkey refused to pay him. "Why!" he exclaimed, "you have shared my dinner, and thanks to me you have three animals in your belly."

The tiger was furious. He cast himself upon the monkey, who with great agility jumped into a tree. Seeing that he could not reach him, the tiger went away swearing to be avenged. He invited all his relatives to a meeting near the stream where they used to drink.

"Let us all band together to prevent the monkey from drinking at this stream," he told his relatives. They all agreed, and camped by the stream.

The monkey waited for a long while before trying to get a drink. But when he could bear his thirst no longer, he thought of a plan. Knowing that he would be devoured by the tiger and his relatives if he approached the stream, he jumped into a barrel which a man was carrying on his cart, certain that it contained water. Lamentably, it was honey.

He was, however, not disheartened. He covered himself well with the honey, then, jumping out of the barrel, he headed for a spot where there was a pile of dry leaves. He rolled over and over in the pile of leaves, until his body was completely covered with leaves.

Thus disguised, he went towards the stream, passing under the very nose of the tiger.

"Hello, leafy!" greeted the tiger cordially, not recognizing the monkey. But the monkey did not reply. He pretended not to hear.

Continuing on his way, the monkey reached the stream, where he drank until he was full. Then he carefully shook off all the leaves with which he was covered and ran full speed past the tiger and his relatives, shouting, *"Piticau, piticau!"*

The tiger became more furious than ever at the trick the monkey had played on him. So he thought of a plan whereby he could deceive the monkey. He dug a large hole in the ground at the very spot where the monkey usually passed. He went into the hole and ordered the other tigers to cover him well with earth, but to leave out his eyes and his large teeth.

When the monkey passed by, he became at once distrustful of this strange sight. "I never saw earth with teeth before," he exclaimed loudly, taking up a large stone, and throwing it at the tiger's teeth, as he ran away. The tiger, seeing that he was frustrated in his attempt to deceive the monkey, also decided to go home.

As for the monkey, mischievous as ever, he continued to play his pranks, and enjoy his tricks; but from that day he and the tiger became enemies.

THE MONKEY AND THE RABBIT

In the days of long ago, when the world was very young, when animals ruled kingdoms, and there was food a-plenty, when birds and beasts frolicked together in seeming harmony, there were none more frolicksome than the monkey and the rabbit.

With not much else to do but play all day, they were constantly seeking new ways to while away the time. And when they had nothing more exciting to do, they would spend their time chasing butterflies.

Then one day, in a moment of mad inspiration, the monkey and the rabbit decided to make their chasing of butterflies a serious affair. With that end in view, they entered into an agreement.

"I," said the monkey, "will kill the butterflies; and you, dear rabbit, will seek them wherever they fall and bring them back to me."

Now, they entered into this agreement at the time when the lion was king of the woods. Every bit a king, he had strictly forbidden his subjects to get out of his sight. All creatures, he commanded, must walk, live, and eat on dry land, and on the ground near him, their king, in order to hear him whenever he called.

The creatures obeyed, one and all. They dared not disobey. They lived on dry land, on the ground, within calling distance of the lion, their king; always ready to fulfil his every wish, answer his every call.

It so happened, that on one occasion during that time, the rabbit fell asleep under the shade of a tree. A little tired he was, perhaps from running errands for his king; a little tired, perhaps from retrieving butterflies for the monkey, his partner. Resting in sleep, with his long ears outstretched, the rabbit looked remarkably like a butterfly. At least, so thought the monkey, who had developed such a passion for hunting butterflies, that he saw them in every shadow. Not perceiving his mistake, the monkey tugged at the ear of his sleeping partner, believing it to be a butterfly.

With a start, the rabbit awoke, only to find the monkey tugging at his ears.

"What a distasteful joke!" the rabbit said in a huff. The monkey said nothing. He offered no explanation, made no apologies. Instead, he laughed merrily, thinking it to be quite funny.

Deeply hurt at the unkind behaviour of his partner, the rabbit swore vengeance.

The opportunity came a few days later, when he found the monkey sitting on a stone with his long tail outstretched, not curled up as was usual. To tell the truth, he found his long tail a nuisance, sometimes. He was never quite sure where it would find itself.

Armed with a stick, the rabbit crept slowly, slowly towards the monkey; and with a sure blow he hit the monkey's tail.

"What a stout vine!" he said as he whacked away.

Screeching shrilly, and out of his mind with pain, the monkey forgot the king's command. Quickly, he clambered into a nearby tree.

Immediately the rabbit was filled with remorse. He reflected on what he had done. Slipping away, he began to sing:

From all guilt
I want to be free,
And so I must live
Always under a tree.

So it was. From that day on, all monkeys climb trees, and rabbits can live only under them, slipping along with short hops, on the ground.

THE MONKEY AND THE WAX DOLL

On the edge of a forest, long, long ago, there lived an old woman and an old man. Not far from their cottage was a banana plantation which they owned. Each morning the old woman would get up before dawn to give the old man his first meal of the day. Then as the sun rose, he would set out with his hoe over his shoulders to the banana plantation, where he worked all day lovingly tending the plants, clearing away the dried leaves, digging the furrows around the roots of the plants, and pulling up the weeds. And each day he watched the plants getting taller and stronger, until one day the first fruits appeared, young and green with purple sheaths at their tips. Happily he went home that evening. "Good wife," he said, "the banana plants have begun to bear fruits." And joyfully he began to make plans for the future.

His wife, too, was overjoyed. She knew how hard he had worked, how carefully he had tended his plants, and now he was rewarded with a very good crop and would have a fine harvest. But before the fruits were ready for reaping, the old man was called away to the city by the king. Immediately. And she found herself alone, in her little cottage, on the edge of the forest, with a banana plantation to tend, only she did not know what to do.

Day after day, she went to the plantation to watch the fruits grow. Soon she saw that it was time for reaping them and since her husband had still not returned, she decided to do it by herself. But the plants were tall and the fruits hanging from the top, and although she tried, she could not reach them. Finally, in frustration, she burst into tears. She was crying bitterly when a monkey, happening to pass by, offered to help her.

He climbed the tree and when he reached the top where the fruits were hanging, he ate the ripe ones, but placed the green ones in the basket which the old woman had given him.

The woman saw that she had been deceived by the clever monkey and swore to make him pay dearly for his trick. But he was agile and astute and he escaped.

"With my own hands I'll overpower him yet," she vowed, and secluded in her house, she put her hands to work. With wax she made the figure of a gigantic doll, fashioning and dressing it to look like a boy. When she had finished, she placed him quite far from her house, hanging on his left arm a basket full of ripe bananas, and placing on his head another basket full of ripe fruits, as if he were a street vendor.

After a while, the monkey appeared on the road, singing while he ate a crust of hard bread. Scarcely had he seen the boy when, believing him to be a fruit vendor, he threw away his crusty stale bread, and ran towards him, demanding a banana. "At once!"

Receiving no reply, he again insisted and becoming impatient because the boy did not reply, he shouted, "Boy, give me a banana or I will slap you." He received no reply. Annoyed at the continued silence, the monkey kept his promise. But on slapping the doll, his hand stuck to the wax.

When the first moment of surprise had passed he shouted again, "Boy, let go of my hand and give me a banana or I will again punish you." Silence followed. Angrily, he again slapped the doll and his other hand stuck to the wax. Becoming now quite furious, he screamed, "Boy, let go of my hands and give me a banana or I will give you a kick!" The boy was quiet ... and the monkey kicked the boy only to have his leg stick to the wax. Shouting now more angrily than ever, the monkey cried, "Boy, let go of my hands and my leg and give me a banana or you will get another kick!" So he said; so he did, and, as was to be expected, his other leg stuck to the wax doll. Completely infuriated, he burst out shouting, "You wretched boy! Let go of my hands and legs, and give me a banana or I'll butt you in your belly." He did, and he became completely stuck to the doll.

The old woman, who had been watching from a hiding place, then thought it safe to approach him. Using a rope which she had plaited from the banana bark, she beat the monkey so soundly that he cried out for mercy. The monkey went away, but sad to say, he never changed his ways.

THE DISDAINFUL GIRL

There lived a beautiful maiden, more beautiful than any other mortal, long, long ago. The most beautiful girl in the land, she was the pride of her parents, and people came from far and near to gaze at her, so lovely was she to look at. But she had one shortcoming, and that is, she was very proud and obstinate.

When the time came for her to be married, as was the custom then, the parents presented one suitor after another, but none of them would she have.

"He is too short, or he is too tall; he is too thin or he is too fat," she would say in proud disdain.

Time went by, and her parents became so angry at the disdainful behaviour of their daughter, that they vowed to give her to anyone who should ask her hand in marriage. The word went round throughout the land.

Not long after this, a great dance was given in the village and to it came visitors from the country round about. Among the visitors, there came a tall and handsome youth, dressed in a flowing robe, elaborately embroidered, and with a ring around his head like a halo. All eyes were drawn to the tall and princely youth, and no one was more attracted to him than the beautiful girl, whose gaze followed him wherever he turned.

He, too, was struck by her great beauty, and asked to dance with her. Lightly and gracefully she whirled around the room, dancing on feet that scarcely touched the floor. Again and again he danced with her. And as the dancing lasted for several days, it was little wonder that at the end of it she had fallen in love with him.

Now the beautiful girl had a brother, who by chance happened to see that the handsome youth had a second mouth at the back of his head. At once, he became suspicious and warned his mother that the young man was not what he seemed. "I smell danger," he said.

"Nonsense!" said his mother. "He is such a fine looking lad! What danger could there be?"

"Ask him his name and where he's from," urged the girl's brother.

"You are just a worrier, suspicious of every stranger," replied the mother, who herself was greatly impressed with the handsome youth, his fine robe and his princely bearing.

"You'll be sorry," said the brother. "I know he is dangerous. Did you see his second mouth?"

The mother was very stern with her son, who after all was young and inexperienced. "You are just imagining things," she said. Crushed, the brother turned away. But he was sure that he was right. Taking his sister aside, he whispered to her, "Do be careful; that handsome stranger is evil." But the girl, obstinate as ever, heeded not his words. So that when the handsome youth asked for her hand in marriage, she was delighted and her parents gladly consented.

The wedding was planned. The marriage celebration was the biggest and most glorious the village had ever known. Laughter and music filled the air, as the whole village feasted and danced day after day, for indeed never before had such a handsome couple been seen.

Before the last dance was danced, the last guest departed from the marriage feast, the young man said to the beautiful girl: "Come now, my bride, with me to the house I have prepared for you." And to the sound of music and dancing, the handsome youth and his bride set out on the journey to his home, many days away.

The brother, still feeling uneasy about the handsome stranger, decided to follow them at a distance. As they got farther and farther away from the village, the girl felt a tinge of sadness descending upon her. Sad she was, at leaving her friends and her parents behind. So to lighten her spirit, to cheer the way, the youth told tales to her as they walked.

"Can you still see the smoke from your parents' house?" he asked after a while.

"Yes, I can," she replied, feeling a bond of closeness with the smoke which came from her parents' house.

Over rocks, over swamps, over plains, over hills, they walked and walked, till again the young man asked: "Can you see the hills behind your parents' house?"

"Yes, I can," she said, happy to see the hills which linked her to her parents' house.

At last, the hills disappeared from view and she could restrain her tears no longer.

"Weep your last tears, my dear. For never more will you see those lovely hills, that friendly smoke which bind you to your parents' house." As he said these words, the halo disappeared from around his head.

Finally, after days of walking, they reached his home on the edge of a forest. It was night. Tired from the long journey, they retired early. During the night, a slight stirring, a stealthy rustle awakened the girl. She awoke to find that the young man had gone from her side. Cowering in terror, she listened to the howling of the hyenas, prowling outside her door, as it seemed to her; the roaring of the lion as it stalked its prey; and the thousand noises heard at night, coming from the dark forest. Terrified, she searched through the house, room after room, for her husband. Not finding him, she cowered, weeping, in a corner farthest from the sound of the howling hyenas.

Towards morning, when the dawn was beginning to break, she heard a rattling sound at her window. Frightened, she looked out, but could see nothing. Timidly, she retreated even farther away, waiting for the comfort of dawn.

Not long afterwards, there was a rattling at the door. "Let me in! Let me in! It is I, your husband," said a voice.

"Do not open," the morning breeze seemed to whisper.

"Let me in! Let me in ..."

Ignoring the warning whisper, she joyfully ran to open the door. Gladly she saw the handsome youth, her husband. Swiftly she flew into his arms, only to recoil in fresh terror at a fleck of blood which spotted his cheeks.

"You are hurt! You are hurt!" she cried in grief.

At the words, his flowing robe fell from his shoulders and he was transformed into a tawny spotted leopard. Fear made her motionless. She could no more move than if she had been a stone. Crouching, with a growl, the leopard prepared to spring on her.

But just at that moment her brother, who, unknown to her, had hidden himself outside the house, and had whispered the warning, played upon the drum he had fashioned while waiting. Glaring ferociously, the animal paused in his tracks, and as the brother continued to play the drum, the leopard remained, transfixed.

The girl, however, came to life at the sound. Gliding safely by the leopard, she was caught up in the arms of her brother, who with the magic of his drum transported her back to her home.

So happy were her parents to see her that they forgot their foolish vow; and the beautiful girl lived, cured forever of her arrogance and pride.

THE MONKEY AND THE CALABASH

The monkey and the tiger were once upon a time good friends. But one day, in a mischievous moment, the monkey played a trick on the tiger, who never quite forgave him for having made a fool of him. From that day on, the monkey went about afraid of his former friend. He never passed tiger's house if he could help it. He never went to the same party as tiger. In fact, he tried to keep out of tiger's way as much as possible.

But one day, there was a fiesta to which the monkey had to go. Sadly, he discovered that the only way to get to it was by passing right in front of tiger's house. How could he get to the fiesta without running into danger, without being seen by tiger? The monkey thought and thought.

He finally found the answer. He put himself into a large calabash, and after giving it a push to start it, he went rolling down the road in complete disguise. He rolled by tiger's house.

Tiger, looking through his door, saw what he believed was a strange new creature. "Who could that stranger be?" he said to himself.

Tiger came out into the road, and looked the stranger up and down. Then he struck up a conversation with the strange animal as he tried to find out who he was. They chatted for a long while, about the weather, about the fiesta, about this and that. But tiger became none the wiser about the identity of the strange creature. Finally they parted very good friends.

The monkey continued on his way, hidden in the calabash, and so happy was he at having escaped tiger's anger that he began to sing as he rolled merrily along:

> *Go on, Calabash, go on!*
> *You never walked before.*
> *Friday, Saturday, Sunday, oh!*
> *You became an animalito*
> *Go on, Calabash, go on*
> *That is what I wanted, oh!*
> *Go on, Calabash, go on!*

And so he arrived at the fiesta without any trouble. There he ate a lot, danced a great deal, had a rollicking time, and made new friends ... until he lost them all because of his wild pranks.

POST SCRIPT

The stories in this collection form part of the rich body of oral tradition[1] which survived in the New World. Although many of these tales are from Brazil, some have variants in islands of the Caribbean and in the southern part of the United States of America.

African tales seemed to have survived in the New World in cycles, depending perhaps, on the cultural origin of the transmitters of the tales, so that Anansi stories abound in Jamaica, stories about Brer Rabbit in the southern part of the United States of America, while in Brazil, the Monkey[2] seems to be the predominant figure.

Except for Haiti[3], Brazil is often considered to be the country in the New World in which elements of African culture survived longest, and this retention occurred, despite the fact that the Jesuits undertook the task of christianizing the Africans as soon as they were brought into the country. Several reasons have been given for this persistence, but only one will be mentioned here.

The Yoruba group, perhaps the most numerous, and certainly the most culturally vital in Brazil, already had an established society with a well defined culture and a complex mythology. Their concept of God as Supreme Being, Creator of the Universe was not completely alien to doctrines preached by the church. In addition, they believed that there were lesser beings, intermediaries between God and Man, known as orishas. These they saw as equivalent to the saints of the Roman Catholic Church, especially as many were seen to be performing similar functions, and since they had rituals and feast days associated with the orishas, they could relate to the ritual and feast days dedicated to the saints. To this day, there are many religious festivals in Brazil which partake of this dual characteristic. This phenomenon of reconciling one religion with another is known as syncretism. Through reconciliation both survived.

It was not so in the Protestant English speaking islands of the Caribbean[4]. The Protestant churches, relatively free of ritual, especially those of the Lutheran and Calvinist faiths, made it more difficult to hold on to the religions of ancient Africa; the mythologies and the gods were forgotten, and the only traces that have remained are at the folk level in the form of various cults, with little understanding of their mythological origin.

The Yoruba creation myth has survived in fragmented form in Brazil, though it is obvious that some of the orishas have been lost, perhaps because they were no longer relevant in the new society, since "a god is a metaphor identifying a personality and an element of nature".[5] Traces of the creation myth are to be found, however, in "The Tortoise and the Fruit."

With the folktales proper,[6] the motifs and themes have remained fairly consistent. But, on comparing variants, it is seen that substitutions are sometimes made, either in the central characters, which may be reflecting the flora and fauna of the country in which the tale is told, or they may be incorporating events or sentiments that are relevant only to that particular society.

An example of character substitution is seen in the tale, "The Monkey and the Wax Doll," as it is told in Brazil, and its better known variant, "Brer Rabbit and the Tar Baby," from the southern part of the United States of America.

"The Monkey and his Tail," also told in Brazil is an example of a folktale incorporating details that reflect the particular flavour of the time and place in which it is told. During the early colonial period of Brazil, the archbishopric of Bahia in Brazil and the archbishopric of Angola in Africa were under the jurisdiction of one archbishop who resided in Bahia, the capital of the country at that time. There was consequently, much trafficking, commercial as well as religious, between the two countries, hence the Monkey's refrain, "To Angola, I'm going."

As far as I have been able to ascertain, the Kebungo, the marsupial type creature who features in, "The Kebungo, the Dog and the Hare," and "The Kebungo and the Boy with the Bag of Feathers," is unknown in the Caribbean. But the latter story may well be taken as an example of the acculturation which must have taken place in Brazil. It is not difficult to see elements of the story of Daedalus and Icarus in "The Kebungo and the Boy with the Bag of Feathers." When and where the influence crept into the story is not known, for the Greeks had knowledge of Africa ages before Europeans came to the New World, and the Portuguese had contact with Africa, first through the Moorish invasion of Portugal, and then through their maritime explorations along the west coast of Africa, long before they settled in Brazil. It would be interesting, of course to find out if this tale exists in Africa, and if so, in what way it departs from the version told in Brazil.

In telling the tales, I have endeavoured to remain faithful to the folktale motifs, adding however, artistic elaborations, some of which were suggested by seeing a performance of the *candomble*[7], a ritual dance performed in a night club in Bahia for the delight of tourists, but nevertheless full of evocation and reminiscent of the ritual dances of all ancient peoples in veneration of their gods, as suppliants of a mysterious being. Then later at the Museu do Homem do Nordeste (Museum of Man of the Northeast) in Recife, I saw exhibits of the material aspects of African culture in Brazil — the kings and queens of carnival dressed in the regalia and finery of the most elegant of European courts[8], the special dishes set aside for each orisha (reminiscent of the 'kosher' dishes of Judaism) and I saw how culture can survive, yet bear the imprint of other cultures, and by so doing create something totally new.

E.F.D.

NOTES

[1]   The Africans who were Moslems had a written literature.
[2]   The stories might have survived too, because of the visible presence in the New World of creatures known in the Old. In Brazil, for example, there are over fifty different varieties of monkeys.
[3]   Generally speaking African culture survived mostly in the Roman Catholic countries of the New World, in Haiti, Brazil, Cuba, Dominican Republic, etc.
[4]   The exception is probably Trinidad where elements of the Yoruba religion have been kept alive by the descendants of Africans who were captured by the English from Spanish slave ships in the 19th century, then given their freedom and permission to settle in the interior of the island.
[5]   Northrop Frye. *The Great Code: The Bible and Literature*. New York and London, Harcourt Brace Janovich Publishers, 1982, p. 37.
[6]   "Stories that tell a society what is important for it to know ... about its gods ... may be called myths ... folktales are told for entertainment ... See Northrop Frye. *Ibid.* p. 33.
[7]   A Brazilian folk ritual of Yoruba cultural origin.
[8]   In 1808 the Portuguese king D. Joao VI removed his court to Brazil to escape Napoleon's invasion of Portugal. He returned to Portugal in 1821 and left his son Pedro I to rule as regent, but in 1822 the Brazilians, wanting to be independent, established an Empire with Pedro I as the first emperor. The Brazilian Empire lasted until 1889 when the country became a Republic.